THE WAY OF
WORSHIP
STUDENT WORKBOOK

THE WAY OF
WORSHIP
STUDENT WORKBOOK

A HANDS-ON GUIDE TO LIVING AND LEADING
AUTHENTIC WORSHIP

MICHAEL NEALE AND
VERNON M. WHALEY

ZONDERVAN

The Way of Worship Student Workbook
Copyright © 2020 by Michael Neale and Vernon M. Whaley

Requests for information should be addressed to:
Zondervan, *3900 Sparks Dr. SE, Grand Rapids, Michigan 49546*

ISBN 978-0-310-10406-3 (softcover)

ISBN 978-0-310-10407-0 (ebook)

Published in association with Verne Kenney.

Cover design: Micah Kandros
Cover art: Shutterstock®
Interior design: Kait Lamphere

Printed in the United States of America

20 21 22 23 24 25 26 27 28 29 30 31 /LSC/ 20 19 18 17 16 15 14 13 12 11 10 9 8 7 6 5 4 3 2 1

CONTENTS

PART 2: PRACTICES

C. HIS POWER, OUR AWARENESS

D. HIS WORK, OUR RELATIONSHIPS

INTRODUCTION

What is worship? What does it mean to be a worshiper and to lead others in worship?

The workbook you hold in your hands is our way of helping you answer that question. When used along with the textbook, *The Way of Worship*, it provides a biblical and practical introduction to help you begin to form a theology of worship. I (Michael) and my dear friend and worship theologian Dr. Vernon M. Whaley invite you to join us on a journey into the Scriptures. In each chapter of *The Way of Worship*, I have briefly narrated a fictional episode of a story inspired by a journey on a river. These stories serve as teaching points, providing helpful metaphors that can be used to unpack the biblical wisdom that inspires and informs our worship of God. Throughout this journey we will uncover new connections between our experiences on the river and the role of worship leaders as we plumb the depths of God's Word and sharpen our minds, quicken our spirits, and learn *The Way of Worship*.

We are excited to share this journey with you. The textbook, *The Way of Worship*, provides a "deeper dive," a more comprehensive and information-rich exposition of worship. But we believe that the contents of that book will be even more helpful when they are paired with this workbook. You will be challenged and encouraged by having someone lead you through each chapter, highlighting crucial connections and guiding you with practical spiritual exercises. You may be using the textbook in a course in which the instructor is supplementing with lectures and additional resources. This workbook can be used as part of such a course as well as by individuals or small groups studying on their own. Designed to complement the textbook, its chapters correspond to the chapters in *The Way of Worship*.

The workbook contains different types of assignments designed to bring home the key idea of each chapter. Sometimes there may be more questions in a chapter than can be covered in a single lesson. Students and their instructors will need to determine which questions are best to answer and how many of them are feasible to meet the specific needs of the course. Some of the questions can be assigned as homework while others can be completed in class individually or in small groups. Or different groups can work on different questions and then share their answers with the larger group.

The workbook follows the format of the textbook with each chapter divided into three sections: Story, Metaphor, and Wisdom. The Story and Metaphor sections utilize "the river" as a metaphor for experiencing God himself. In some traditions, water or rivers have symbolized the working of the Holy Spirit in the life of the believer. In this book we are using "the river" to represent the person of God himself as Father, Son (Jesus Christ), and Holy Spirit. Rivers in Scripture often communicate important insights about God, redemption, and worship.

It is in Genesis that the word *river* appears for the first time in the Bible. The Bible goes into great detail to describe perfect worship with a perfect God in a perfect place, Garden of Eden. The author specifically points out that a river flowed through Eden and watered the garden. There are many other important rivers throughout the scriptural narrative. There are no less than 148 references to a river or rivers involving God's plan for his people after the first river mentioned in Genesis 2:10. When God makes a covenant with Abram, he marks out the boundaries of the promised land by the river of Egypt and the Euphrates.[1] Moses' very name relates the story of how his mother saved his life by setting him afloat on the river in a papyrus basket.[2] Job drinks of the river water from the Jordan.[3] Psalm 1 compares a man who fears God to a tree planted by the river. Again, the psalmist compares God's provisions to a flowing river. Psalm 46 says there is a river that brings joy to the heavenly city, where the true source of security is God himself.[4] The prophets Jeremiah, Ezekiel, Joel, and Daniel all employ rivers as metaphors for God's provision.[5] Zechariah and Daniel's visions include a river. Jesus was baptized in a river,[6] and he describes the Holy Spirit being like a river in the believer's heart.[7] The disciples baptized the first Christians in a river,[8] and Paul prays by the riverside.[9] John sees a pure river of water of life in his great eschatological vision, described in Revelation.[10]

The river is a symbol of life. In Genesis, "a river" flows from Eden, the source of all life and relationships, and then splits into four different streams that water the nations. The river in heaven flows from the throne of God. Rivers represent God's provisions to sustain, love, and care for his own creation—including you and me.

This provision and relationship is what we will investigate throughout the pages of this book. Relationship with a holy God, through Jesus Christ, is at the heart of our worship and the basis for our worship leading. Some of the questions in the workbook ask you to look up passages of Scripture to answer a specific question. Others may require more personal reflections about the issues raised in the chapter. The goal is to help you apply the wisdom uncovered in your reading by personally applying it to your own life and worship leadership. The content of the Wisdom sections, in particular, will target several of the essential issues facing those of us leading worship every week. Twenty-eight strategic "heart issues" are dealt with and discussed as they relate to the joy of worship.

We hope and pray that the Lord will use the textbook and this accompanying workbook to encourage, challenge, and help you mature and grow as both a worshiper and leader of worship.

Michael Neale
Vernon M. Whaley

A. HIS REVELATION, OUR RESPONSE

CHAPTER 1

HIS PLAN

God's purposes for worship are revealed from Genesis to Revelation.

STORY

"I don't believe in accidents. The canyon walls. The wildlife. The sky. The river and how it carves out the earth and brings life to the lowest places. Us. There's a plan for us. We are here with the river today, experiencing her in all her glory. We have a place in it all. There's evidence of a plan. A greater story."

1. Think about your own story. When did you first sense that God had a greater plan for your life?

_____

_____

_____

_____

2. Describe a time when you hoped to know God's specific plan, but it wasn't clear to you.

_____

_____

_____

3. At that particular time, did it become clear? If so, how?

_____

_____

_____

_____

_____

4. Name and describe three defining moments in your life that at first seemed like detours but in hindsight you see the plan of God was at work (i.e., a move to another city, a teacher encouraged you, a new job opportunity, etc.).

_____

_____

_____

_____

_____

METAPHOR

"Remember the former things, those of long ago;
  I am God, and there is no other;
  I am God, and there is none like me.
I make known the end from the beginning,
  from ancient times, what is still to come.
I say, 'My purpose will stand,
  and I will do all that I please.'"
—ISAIAH 46:9–10

God makes known the end from the beginning. He is writing the story of the ages, *his*tory.

1. If God is truly writing the story of history, how should this affect our decision-making process?

_____

_____

_____

_____

2. If you were to draw a road map to a successful, God-honoring life, what would that look like? Try to put it in five to seven stages, like stops on a road trip (i.e., finish education, friendships, marriage, career, etc.).

_____

_____

_____

_____

_____

_____

3. What are the most important things to you to achieve in life?

_____

_____

_____

_____

4. What do you believe are the most important things to God for your life?

_____

_____

_____

_____

WISDOM

1. God is a God of *relationship, revelation, and redemption*: How does God provide a way for relationship with man?

_____

_____

_____

_____

2. How does God reveal himself and his plans for mankind? Be specific.

_____

_____

_____

_____

3. How does revelation help worshipers to know, understand, and find God?

_____

_____

_____

_____

4. How does mankind respond to God's revelation?

_____

_____

_____

_____

5. God is a God of *redemption*. How does relationship and revelation present God's plan for redemption?

_____

_____

_____

_____

6. What are some of the benefits of redemption for the person seeking to know the way of worship?

_____

_____

_____

CHAPTER 2

HIS CALL

The Spirit is calling us to relationship to and worship of him!

STORY

"The river called me, for sure . . . I belong to the waters. It's like the waters chose me to be here, to revel in the beauty and power, and to guide others to do the same. I couldn't really think about being anywhere else or doing anything else."

Michael: I was nine years old when a revival evangelist named Roger Mullins spoke on a Sunday evening at our seventy-five-member church. It was during his message that I got a glimpse of what Jesus did for me. I sensed that I had been chosen to be a child of God. He wanted me. It was at the same altar call that night I also sensed a vocational call to ministry. I didn't know exactly what that would look like, but God did. I shed many tears at the call of God's love to me that night.

1. When and where did God call you to be his child? What was the day of your salvation?

_____

_____

_____

_____

_____

2. Describe the details surrounding that moment. Who was with you? What was happening? What did you feel? Did someone lead you to trust Christ as Savior? If so, who was it?

_____

_____

_____

_____

3. Have you been called (or do you feel called) to vocational ministry? In what area (music, the arts, preaching, missions, etc.)?

_____

_____

_____

_____

4. How did God speak to you about this calling? Through someone or something?

_____

_____

_____

_____

5. Describe what you sense God is calling you to do in both broad and specific terms.

_____

_____

_____

_____

6. Why do you think God called you to do this?

_____

_____

_____

_____

7. Who are the people in your life that have shaped your calling?

_____

_____

_____

_____

METAPHOR

Then I heard the voice of the Lord saying, "Whom shall I send? And who will go for us?"

And I said, "Here am I. Send me!"

—ISAIAH 6:8

1. Read Isaiah 6:1–8 and in each verse describe either what Isaiah sees or what occurs when God calls him.

v. 1

_____

_____

_____

_____

v. 2

_____

_____

_____

_____

v. 3

_____

_____

_____

_____

v. 4

_____

_____

_____

v. 5

_____
_____
_____
_____

v. 6

_____
_____
_____
_____

v. 7

_____
_____
_____
_____

v. 8

_____
_____
_____
_____

2. God's call brings us to salvation. His call brings us to relationship. His call brings us to our purpose. His call brings us to our ministry. What is another metaphor you could use for responding to the call of God on your life?

_____
_____
_____
_____

3. In the Story (see page 17), the river called to John, our whitewater guide. How did he respond?

_____
_____
_____
_____

4. What are some potential distractions in your life after hearing the call?

_____

_____

_____

_____

5. What are some counterfeit callings you may be tempted to settle for?

_____

_____

_____

_____

_____

WISDOM

1. In what ways would you say that the calling is very personal?

_____

_____

_____

_____

2. God's calling is a vital part of his planned purposes. How have you seen that to be true in your life? Or in the lives of the men and women leading worship that you respect and admire?

_____

_____

_____

_____

3. God's calling involves a twofold process. Part one is to *recognize* the call. How do you think a worshiper can recognize the call?

_____

_____

_____

_____

4. Part two is to immediately *respond* to the call. When God calls, the worshiper's responsibility is to obey without delay. What are ways that you can recognize and respond to God's call through obedience?

_____

_____

_____

_____

5. How did the following people respond to the call of God?

Abraham (Genesis 12:1–9; 22)

_____

_____

_____

Moses (Exodus 3–4)

_____

_____

_____

Joshua (Joshua 1:1–9; 5:13–15; 6)

_____

_____

_____

Samuel, as a child hearing God (1 Samuel 3)

_____

_____

_____

Isaiah, when seeing the Lord high and lifted up (Isaiah 6:8)

_____

_____

_____

Jesus in the garden (Matthew 26:36–46)

_____

_____

_____

Paul on the Damascus road (Acts 9:1–31)

_____

_____

_____

6. In what ways can you give testimony that God's calling on a person's life is powerful, persistent, and personal?

_____

_____

_____

_____

7. Why can't someone else receive God's calling on your behalf?

_____

_____

_____

CHAPTER 3

THE CENTER

God is the center of all things, we are not.

STORY

"You are not the center, John. The river is the center. It was here before you and it will be here when you are gone. Remember, John; we were made for the river, not the other way around. The river does not need us, John. We need the river. Life, energy, joy, beauty, vitality, purpose, it's all in the river. Someday, you will see, and then you will tell your sons and daughters."

1. Describe a moment and story from your life when all you really cared about was one thing, and that one thing consumed you.

_____

_____

_____

_____

2. Name three lead characters in Scripture who revealed that God was not the center of their existence but someone or something else was (i.e., the rich young ruler).

_____

_____

_____

_____

3. When Jesus is the center of our lives, how does that practically affect our time
    and resources?

    _____

    _____

    _____

    _____

4. When Jesus is the center of our lives, how does that affect how we relate to others?
    Consider family, friends, coworkers, and teammates, specifically.

    _____

    _____

    _____

    _____

    _____

METAPHOR

After reading Colossians 1:9–18, complete the following guide skills tasks:

1. Ask the Holy Spirit to reveal the things that are consuming your attentions.
    Is it something you are worried about? Is it something you are striving for?
    Write it down like this:

    My _achievement_ is not the center, Jesus; you are the center.

    My _song_ is not the center, Jesus; you are the center.

    My _idea_ is not the center, Jesus; you are the center.

    My _____ is not the center, Jesus; you are the center.

    My _____ is not the center, Jesus; you are the center.

    My _____ is not the center, Jesus; you are the center.

    My _____ is not the center, Jesus; you are the center.

2. Take a few minutes each morning to commit your thoughts, ambitions, goals, aspirations, and heart's desires to the Lord!

_____

_____

_____

_____

_____

3. List ten attributes of God that are magnificent and nearly indescribable.

_____

_____

_____

_____

_____

_____

_____

_____

_____

_____

_____

_____

4. Sing to God in the quiet, just you, and ask God to allow his presence to wash **over you.**

_____

_____

_____

_____

_____

WISDOM

1. Describe in twenty-five words or less the time you began to comprehend that Jesus **must be** the center of your worship.

_____

_____

_____

_____

2. In what ways do you *practice* comprehending and acknowledging Jesus as the center of all?

_____

_____

_____

_____

3. In what ways do you make Jesus the center—the most important aspect of your own personal and public times of worship?

_____

_____

_____

_____

_____

4. Describe ways you are tempted to displace Jesus from the center of your life and worship. (It could be someone, something—any idol that is fashioned in his place.)

_____

_____

_____

_____

_____

5. Anything other than Jesus as the absolute center of our lives always distorts our perception and vision of who we are. How have you noticed your priorities or vision becoming distorted when Jesus is not the absolute center of your life?

_____

_____

_____

_____

_____

6. If we are only successful when recognizing that Jesus already has preeminence (the central place) in all of life, how can we guard our hearts against believing other things are more important than Jesus?

_____

_____

_____

_____

CHAPTER 4

AWE AND WONDER

Cultivate an awareness and awe of the wonder of God's
love, his creation, and his work in the world.

STORY

Nature's sacred cathedral was breathtaking. Nothing mattered in those moments
except to behold the beauty, the majesty, and the splendor of the river.

John breathed deeply through his nose and lifted his face to the sky, his
eyes closed against the radiance of the sun.

"You smell that? It's peace. It's beauty. I never tire of it. The river has
been carving this canyon for thousands of years. It carries life to the valley.
It sustains everything around here. Incredible, isn't it?"

"It's magnificent," Leah said under her breath.

"It's mysterious and powerful and it never fails to show me something I
haven't seen before," John continued to muse. "Inexhaustible treasures are
in the river, that's what I always say."

1. Describe a time you were overcome with awe and wonder. Remember specific
details of where you were, what you saw, what it felt like, and how it impacted you.

_____

_____

_____

_____

2. Explore the five following Bible passages in which someone was struck with awe and wonder in the presence of God. Fill in the character, incident, and response for each (an example has been provided).

Passage	Character	Incident	Response
Isaiah 6	Isaiah	vision from God	"Woe is me!"

METAPHOR

1. Name three of your favorite outdoor activities.

_____

_____

_____

_____

2. Describe the most dangerous thing you've ever done.

_____

_____

_____

_____

3. In what ways do you experience the beauty of God? (e.g., music, film, nature) Note a few and explain why you love them so much.

_____

_____

_____

WISDOM

1. Read and meditate on Psalm 16:2, 5–9, 11. Then answer the following questions based on verses 5–9:

How is God your portion and cup? (v. 5)

_____

_____

_____

_____

What inheritance does God provide? (v. 6)

_____

_____

_____

_____

How does God counsel and instruct you? (v. 7)

_____

_____

_____

Why do you keep your eyes on the Lord? (v. 8)

_____

_____

_____

In what way should you respond to God's goodness? (v. 9)

_____

_____

_____

2. Practice meditating (contemplate, ponder, consider, reflect, or muse) on the Lord:

Meditate on the Lord on your bed, before going to sleep. (Psalm 63:6a)

_____

_____

_____

_____

Meditate on the Lord and his Word in the morning. (Psalm 5:3; 30:5c; 59:16; 90:14; 92:2; and 119:148)

_____

_____

_____

_____

Meditate on the Lord "in the night watches." (Psalm 63:6b)

_____

_____

_____

_____

Meditate by singing your favorite song about trusting in the Lord. (Psalm 77:6)

_____

_____

_____

_____

3. Using Psalm 145:1–5 as primary source material, create a short love song to the Lord.

_____

_____

_____

_____

_____

_____

4. Read and meditate on Psalm 95:1–2, 6. Complete the following invitations to worship:

    a. Let us sing _____ (v. 1).
    b. Let us shout _____ (v. 1).
    c. Let us come _____ (v. 2).
    d. Let us extol _____ (v. 2).
    e. Let us bow down _____ (v. 6).
    f. Let us kneel _____ (v. 6).

5. Meditate on Psalm 95:3–5, 7 and think about God's greatness. Take time to worship God and proclaim that:

The Lord is great! (List ways in which he is great.)

_____
_____
_____
_____
_____

The Lord is King and above all gods! (List ways in which the Lord is King.)

_____
_____
_____
_____

In the Lord's hand are the depths of the earth! (List ways in which the Lord's hand are the depth of the earth.)

_____
_____
_____
_____

The mountain peaks belong to the Lord. (In what ways do the mountains peaks belong to the Lord?)

_____
_____
_____
_____

The sea belongs to the Lord. (In what ways do the seas belong to the Lord?)

_____

_____

_____

_____

The Lord's hands formed the dry land. (List ways the Lord's hands form the dry land.)

_____

_____

_____

_____

6. Meditate on these "action phrases" in Psalm 145:1–5.

<u>Think about</u> all the ways the Lord is great and worthy of praise.

_____

_____

_____

_____

<u>Give some examples</u> of how one generation may commend the work of God to another generation.

_____

_____

_____

_____

<u>Think about</u> and list at least three ways you can meditate on the wonderful works of God.

_____

_____

_____

CHAPTER 5

SPIRIT AND TRUTH

The Father is seeking true worshipers; biblical worship engages our spirit (our emotions), biblical worship is based on truth (the Word of God).

STORY

"Hydrology. It's the study of the properties of water and its movement on the earth and in the atmosphere. I believe science and beauty are interwoven. If I just know the data but don't experience the beauty of the river, I might as well be in a lab somewhere. If all I did was run the river without knowledge of its nature or what's actually happening in the canyon, I miss the depth of the experience . . . the truth. Truth fuels my sense of awe and vice versa. You gotta have both if you really want to experience all the river has to offer."

1. List twenty attributes or characteristics of God with a brief definition of each. (e.g., holy, sovereign, etc.)

_____

_____

_____

_____

_____

_____

_____

_____

_____

_____

_____

_____

_____

_____

_____

_____

_____

_____

_____

_____

_____

2. Pick two of those attributes and, using a concordance, list a corresponding Scripture passage where he reveals himself that way.

_____

_____

_____

_____

3. Our guide said, "Truth fuels my sense of awe." Describe a time in your life when you worshiped God as a response to him revealing one of his attributes to you.

_____

_____

_____

_____

METAPHOR

"Yet a time is coming and has now come when the true worshipers will worship the Father in the Spirit and in truth, for they are the kind of worshipers the Father seeks. God is spirit, and his worshipers must worship in the Spirit and in truth."

—JOHN 4:23–24

Our spirit is made up of three components: our mind, will, and emotions.

1. Name three ways we can worship God with our mind.

_____

_____

_____

_____

2. Name three ways we can worship God with our will.

_____

_____

_____

_____

3. Name three ways we can worship God with our emotions.

_____

_____

_____

_____

WISDOM

1. There are two essential elements in worship of God: "the Spirit and truth." In one or two sentences, describe what it means to worship "in the Spirit."

_____

_____

_____

_____

2. What did God breathe into man at creation: the Holy Spirit or the human spirit? Explain the difference.

_____

_____

_____

_____

_____

3. Because God is Spirit, in what way is it his deep desire for all the world to seek him and worship him?

_____

_____

_____

_____

4. In what ways does our spirit represent the image of God?

_____

_____

_____

_____

5. Complete the following statement: I might obtain or welcome the "Holy Spirit" into my life by . . .

Recognizing _____

Realizing _____

Receiving _____

CHAPTER 6

HIS WORD

To know God is to know and feed on his Word.

STORY

He opened up the waterproof satchel and pulled out a two-inch-thick, leather-bound book. It looked nearly antique . . .

"These are generational writings about the river from my family. It's got anecdotes, wisdom, learnings, stories; it's a treasure."

"Wow, I can't believe you bring this out on the water with you." I felt like I was holding something sacred.

"Don't worry, I've got the originals locked away. This is a copy my father made and I've kept using. It never leaves my side. It's my guidebook. I eat the words like food. It's my connection to the past and the bigger story unfolding. It's my connection to the river."

1. Do you have a family heirloom or something you treasure greatly that was passed down to you? If so, describe it.

_____

_____

_____

_____

_____

2. What is the story behind the heirloom?

_____

_____

_____

_____

_____

3. How was it given to you, and why does it mean so much to you?

_____

_____

_____

_____

_____

4. What is the longest you've gone without food, possibly for a fast?

_____

_____

_____

_____

METAPHOR

Your word is a lamp for my feet,
   a light on my path.
                    —PSALM 119:105

For the word of God is alive and active. Sharper than any double-edged sword, it penetrates even to dividing soul and spirit, joints and marrow; it judges the thoughts and attitudes [or intents] of the heart.
                    —HEBREWS 4:12

1. How is the word of God alive and active in your life?

_____

_____

_____

_____

2. Describe a time when you read the Word of God and found that it actually read you.

_____

_____

_____

_____

3. What Scripture passage has convicted you? Record it below.

_____

_____

_____

_____

4. What Scripture passage has given you hope? Record it below.

_____

_____

_____

_____

5. What Scripture passage has given you peace? Record it below.

_____

_____

_____

_____

6. What Scripture passage has given you strength? Record it below.

_____

_____

_____

_____

7. What Scripture passage has changed how you viewed the world around you? Record it below.

_____

_____

_____

8. What Scripture passage has caused you to erupt in praise? Record it below.

_____

_____

_____

_____

9. What Scripture passage has caused you to bow in reverence? Record it below.

_____

_____

_____

_____

10. What Scripture passage has compelled you to lift up the "least of these"? Record it below.

_____

_____

_____

_____

WISDOM

1. There are two essential elements in worship of God: "spirit and truth." In one or two sentences, describe what it means to worship in "truth."

_____

_____

_____

_____

_____

2. In your opinion, what is the difference between worshiping in the Spirit and worshiping in truth?

_____

_____

_____

_____

3. According to our study, there are three types of truth. What are those three types, and how do they relate to the way of worship?

_____

_____

_____

_____

4. How does God reveal himself to man?

_____

_____

_____

_____

5. How is God's truth different than any other concept of truth? Why is this important to the way of worship?

_____

_____

_____

_____

6. What does it really mean to worship God in the Spirit *and* truth?

_____

_____

_____

_____

7. What are the implications of all truth coming from God? How does that affect the way we worship?

_____

_____

_____

_____

8. How does a person worship in truth? How does that apply to your praise-and-worship team?

_____

_____

_____

CHAPTER 7

THANKFULNESS

The cornerstone of a worshiper's heart is a grateful heart.

STORY

Our guide's reply is etched in my memory.

"I know I'm grateful to be here. I'm grateful this is my office." He gazed at the epic scenery all around as he continued. "I'm thankful the river chose me. I'm thankful to meet new people every day, have air in my lungs, and a bright future. I think gratitude is the foundation for peace and joy, so I try to stay in that place."

We all sat silently and drank in the view.

1. In no particular order, list as many things as you can think of that you are thankful for in your life.

_____

_____

_____

_____

_____

_____

_____

_____

_____

2. Describe a time when someone expressed their gratitude to you.

_____

_____

_____

_____

_____

3. How did that make you feel?

_____

_____

_____

_____

_____

4. Describe a time when you realized you lacked thankfulness.

_____

_____

_____

_____

5. How do you avoid becoming ungrateful?

_____

_____

_____

_____

METAPHOR

Give thanks to the LORD, for he is good;
his love endures forever.
—PSALM 118:1

Therefore, since we are receiving a kingdom that cannot be shaken, let us
be thankful, and so worship God acceptably with reverence and awe, for our
"God is a consuming fire."
—HEBREWS 12:28–29

1. What are some ways you foster thankfulness?

_____

_____

_____

_____

_____

2. List five attributes of God you are thankful for and use a metaphor to describe each one. (e.g., his cleansing power and forgiveness, God is a consuming and purifying fire, etc.)

_____

_____

_____

_____

_____

_____

3. Describe a time when you've given God thanks, even when you didn't feel like it.

_____

_____

_____

_____

_____

_____

4. What did you experience on the other side of that obedience?

_____

_____

_____

_____

WISDOM

1. In your own words, describe the attitude and action in Psalm 118:1.

_____

_____

_____

_____

2. What do you think the apostle Paul means when he says to "give thanks in all circumstances" (1 Thessalonians 5:18)?

_____

_____

_____

_____

3. How are gratitude and attitude action words?

_____

_____

_____

_____

4. How does gratitude strengthen relationships?

_____

_____

_____

_____

5. How does gratitude help create a humble spirit?

_____

_____

_____

_____

6. How is gratitude a choice? And why is that choice important?

_____

_____

_____

_____

7. Finally, historically and biblically, gratitude is an important part of our daily walk with God. With this statement in mind, what "attitude outcomes" would *you* think necessary for a worship leader?

_____

_____

_____

_____

B. HIS PURPOSES, OUR OBEDIENCE

CHAPTER 8

TIME

To know God is to spend time with him in prayer and meditation.

STORY

"This is home for me, so I'm always at the river. If you are only here in the summer, you definitely get to experience the river, but there's so much more . . . If you are here year-round, the river shows off in ways you just don't get otherwise. Tourists run the river in the summer; river guides, who really know the river, live here. The river speaks to me through every season. Some of the most beautiful scenes are only experienced in the harshest conditions. There are no shortcuts. It takes time . . . time with the river. There's nowhere else I'd rather be anyway."

1. Has there ever been a season in your life when you realized you had been distracted from what matters most?

_____

_____

_____

2. What kinds of things can distract us from our time with the Lord?

_____

_____

_____

3. Time is our most important commodity. Describe methods that help you budget your time well.

_____

_____

_____

4. If you knew that being with a certain person who loved you unconditionally would give you peace, power, and purpose, how much time of your day/week/month would you give them?

_____

_____

_____

5. Who do you spend the most time with in any given week? Your spouse? Your children? Your coworkers?

_____

_____

_____

6. List a few people you enjoy being with and describe the way you spend time with them.

_____

_____

_____

_____

_____

_____

METAPHOR

As Jesus and his disciples were on their way, he came to a village where a woman named Martha opened her home to him. She had a sister called Mary, who sat at the Lord's feet listening to what he said. But Martha was distracted by all the preparations that had to be made. She came to him and asked, "Lord, don't you care that my sister has left me to do the work by myself? Tell her to help me!"

"Martha, Martha," the Lord answered, "you are worried and upset about many things, but few things are needed—or indeed only one. Mary has chosen what is better, and it will not be taken away from her."
—LUKE 10:38–42

1. What are some tangible ways you can make time to "sit at the feet" of Jesus?

_____

_____

_____

_____

2. Much of prayer is listening to the Lord. Describe a time when you were quiet before the Lord and he spoke to your spirit. What did he say? What happened as a result?

_____

_____

_____

_____

3. Singing and praying the Psalms is a powerful way to spend time with the Lord. If you are worried, what psalm could you make melody with and sing to the Lord? Write it down and sing it with a melody of your own.

_____

_____

_____

_____

4. Do the same for the following categories:

Thankful

_____

_____

_____

_____

Fearful

_____

_____

_____

_____

Excited

_____
_____
_____
_____

Sad

_____
_____
_____
_____

Confused

_____
_____
_____

Weak

_____
_____
_____

WISDOM

1. Jesus delights in spending time with you and me because he wants a relationship with us. How can we establish a relationship with Jesus?

_____
_____
_____
_____

2. What are the benefits of spending time with Jesus?

_____
_____
_____

3. Each person is given the same number of hours in a day to steward. How can we steward the time that God has given us?

_____

_____

_____

4. Write core meaning of Psalm 27:1–5 in your own words.

_____

_____

_____

5. According to this chapter, it is important for worshipers to "set aside a special time and place to be with Jesus." Why is this important? What time of day do you prefer to set aside for time with Jesus?

_____

_____

_____

_____

6. What helps you spend time alone with Jesus? How do you make sure you protect that time?

_____

_____

_____

_____

7. The Bible instructs us in Ephesians 5:16 and Colossians 4:5 to "redeem the time." What does that mean, and why is it important?

_____

_____

_____

_____

8. How have you seen "time with Jesus" transform you and impact the way you live your life?

_____

_____

_____

_____

CHAPTER 9

CHARACTER

Whose you are: stay true to the values of a biblical worshiper and guide.

STORY

"My grandpa used to say, 'What you see isn't always what you get.' That tree looked good on the outside, but the inside told a different story. You apply some pressure and because of the rot, it lets you down."

"That sounds like a people lesson too," I commented.

"Exactly." John got more intense as he pulled a cooler out of the raft. "Character is all. While you have to take care of your body to run the river, what is inside—your core, your values—that's everything. My grandpa also said, 'If you don't stand for something, you'll fall for anything.' If you don't have character, you don't have anything."

1. List five historical figures who lacked character. How did you identify them?

_____

_____

_____

_____

_____

_____

_____

_____

2. Think of someone you know who you believe exhibited a **lack of character**. Without naming them here, list some behaviors that caused you **to believe this.**

_____

_____

_____

_____

_____

3. How did it make you feel to interact with this person? Could **you trust them?**

_____

_____

_____

_____

4. Would you follow them in any given journey or adventure **in life?**

_____

_____

_____

_____

5. Think of someone you know who has exemplary character. Describe **the ways you** recognize their good character.

_____

_____

_____

_____

METAPHOR

For this very reason, make every effort to add to your faith goodness; and to goodness, knowledge; and to knowledge, self-control; and to self-control, perseverance; and to perseverance, godliness; and to godliness, mutual affection; and to mutual affection, love. For if you possess these qualities in increasing measure, they will keep you from being ineffective and unproductive in your knowledge of our Lord Jesus Christ.

—2 PETER 1:5–8

1. Think of the building blocks of a house of exemplary character. Sketch it like a house, starting with the foundation, walls, and so on.

_____

_____

_____

_____

_____

_____

2. Why is character so important for leaders, specifically?

_____

_____

_____

_____

3. List three ways you can protect your character (consider Nehemiah).

_____

_____

_____

_____

4. Pray and ask the Holy Spirit to reveal potential cracks or weaknesses in the structure of your character.

_____

_____

_____

_____

WISDOM

1. Write out a one- or two-sentence definition of the word *character*.

_____

_____

_____

2. Famous poet and author Ralph Waldo Emerson said, "Men of character are the conscience of the society to which they belong."[1] What do you think this statement means?

_____

_____

_____

_____

_____

_____

3. How is character built, fortified, and protected?

_____

_____

_____

_____

_____

4. How does worship affect character building?

_____

_____

_____

_____

_____

5. Which fruits of the Spirit (Galatians 5:22–23) would you like to focus on developing right now?

_____

_____

_____

_____

_____

6. Think of a time God used difficult circumstances to develop character in your life. What did you learn?

_____

_____

_____

_____

_____

7. Abraham Lincoln said, "Character is like a tree and reputation like a shadow. The shadow is what we think of it; the tree is the real thing."[2] What do you think that means?

_____

_____

_____

_____

8. Why is authenticity a critical quality for a worship leader?

_____

_____

_____

_____

9. Read the story about the great composer Franz Joseph Haydn in the corresponding textbook chapter this week. How can you model Haydn's attitude and posture in your own life?

_____

_____

_____

_____

CHAPTER 10

FRESH ENCOUNTERS

Relational worship procures fresh encounters with Jesus.

STORY

"How deep is that water?" I asked John.

"Deep enough to jump in!" John said gleefully.

"Come on, we'll go together!" I looked at Leah.

She peered over the steady swirl below.

"There's all kinds of ways to encounter the river. It's never the same. You've gotta be all in. Just jump and let the current take you back down to where we put the raft out," John said.

After we both got courage up, we grabbed hands and leapt off the rocky ledge.

The cold water took our breath away as we plunged in. It carried us gently downstream. Immediately, our experience with the river went deeper, literally and figuratively. The fear lessened. We were connected in a fresh way.

1. Describe a time or event in your life that was new and exciting. (e.g., a trip to a new place, a visit to a theme park, the making of a new friend, etc.)

_____

_____

_____

_____

2. What made it so memorable to you? Tell us the details: who was there, what was the weather like?

_____

_____

_____

_____

3. Do you like to take risks? Why or why not?

_____

_____

_____

_____

4. Routines and habits are good. But those routines can turn into ruts. Describe one of your physical routines and a way you keep that routine from developing into a rut.

_____

_____

_____

_____

5. Now do the same with a spiritual routine.

_____

_____

_____

_____

METAPHOR

Deep calls to deep
    in the roar of your waterfalls;
all your waves and breakers
    have swept over me.
By day the LORD directs his love,
    at night his song is with me—
    a prayer to the God of my life.
        —PSALM 42:7–8

1. How have you experienced the transforming presence of the Holy Spirit?

_____

_____

_____

_____

_____

2. Find a "fresh encounter" that happened in Scripture. Which one did you pick?

_____

_____

_____

_____

_____

3. Describe the encounter in your own words.

_____

_____

_____

_____

_____

4. What were the conditions that precipitated the encounter with God?

_____

_____

_____

_____

_____

5. What happened as a result of the encounter?

_____

_____

_____

_____

6. What parallels do you see in the scriptural encounter and the one in your own life?

_____

_____

_____

_____

7. List five ways you are hungry to encounter the Lord in this season of life.

WISDOM

1. How have you seen God use worship to shape or form you?

2. What does it mean to have a fresh encounter?

3. How does one have a fresh encounter?

4. What are the three very basic ingredients for us to use in establishing a regular, fresh encounter with God?

5. Psalm 96 provides a practical fivefold outline for experiencing God's goodness and for practicing worship. What are the major ideas that help us know how to do this?

    a. Practice _____ to the Lord a new _____ (vv. 1–2).
    b. Proclaim his _____ among the heathen (vv. 3–6).
    c. Give to the _____ (vv. 7–8).
    d. Enter his _____ (vv. 9).
    e. Feed on his _____ (vv. 10–13).

6. According to Psalm 100, how should we respond to a fresh encounter?

_____

_____

_____

CHAPTER II

BROKENNESS

It is often during deep times of testing that character is shaped and brokenness is transformed into hearts (and lives) of worship.

STORY

"I hear you, man. It happens. You know that feeling you have right now in your gut? Don't forget it. That brokenness will carve the awareness of your need right into your soul. Sometimes it's our own doing, sometimes it's from someone else's stupidity, and sometimes it's just life. Broken is broken. You probably had a weaker paddler on one side that didn't dig in. Stay low. Grow. Prepare. Revere the river. I think if you don't stay broken, it has a way of breaking you. Staying broken hurts less than being broken. As you can see, the stakes are high."

1. We live in a fallen world. List three world events in recent history that remind you of the brokenness of mankind.

_____

_____

_____

_____

_____

_____

2. In Scripture, list three different people who God met in their brokenness.

   _____

   _____

   _____

   _____

   _____

3. How did God respond to the brokenness of each?

   _____

   _____

   _____

   _____

4. Think of a time when you were acutely aware of your brokenness because of circumstances out of your control. (Maybe someone committed a sin against you, or a tragedy struck your family, etc.) Record it here.

   _____

   _____

   _____

   _____

5. Ask God to reveal how he showed up in the midst of that difficulty.

   _____

   _____

   _____

   _____

6. Think of a time when you were acutely aware of your brokenness due to choices you made. Record it here.

   _____

   _____

   _____

   _____

7. Identify a parallel passage of Scripture that speaks into that situation. How did God show up in the Scriptures?

   _____

   _____

   _____

   _____

METAPHOR

Let me hear joy and gladness;
    let the bones you have crushed rejoice.
        —PSALM 51:8

My sacrifice, O God, is a broken spirit;
    a broken and contrite heart
    you, God, will not despise.
        —PSALM 51:17

1. Can you think of a time that God took your brokenness and turned it into something beautiful?

_____

_____

_____

_____

2. What does brokenness produce in our lives if we allow it?

_____

_____

_____

_____

3. In what ways can we stay broken before the Lord?

_____

_____

_____

_____

4. Describe an event in Scripture where God took someone's brokenness and turned it to something beautiful.

_____

_____

_____

_____

WISDOM

1. How does brokenness change our attitude toward God? Toward circumstances? Toward other people? Toward your own, personal worship?

_____

_____

_____

_____

_____

2. What does it mean to be broken in spirit? Why do you think God desires us to be broken in spirit?

_____

_____

_____

_____

_____

3. What is the relationship between pride and brokenness?

_____

_____

_____

_____

_____

4. The Bible declares that "haughty eyes and a proud heart—the unplowed field of the wicked—produce sin" (Proverbs 21:4). Have you ever experienced God removing pride and arrogance from your life through brokenness? Explain.

_____

_____

_____

_____

_____

5. Why is brokenness and being stripped of pride especially important for worship leaders?

_____

_____

_____

6. Brokenness often gives us opportunity to restore fractured relationships. Are there fractured relationships in your life that you would like the Holy Spirit to heal? How can you help in that process? Explain.

_____

_____

_____

_____

7. God uses the brokenness experience to transform us and shape us into better, more effective worship leaders. How do you think you need to humble yourself so that servant leadership becomes a way of life?

_____

_____

_____

_____

CHAPTER 12

HUMILITY

Humility: Absolute removal of selfishness and pride.

STORY

After a few minutes of taking in the magnificent view, we headed back. As we arrived at the beach, we found John putting the final touches on lunch for us. I was taken aback by his attention to detail and hospitality.

"Wow man, thanks for this," I commented quietly to John. "We could've helped."

His reply stuck with me.

"No way, man, I just want you guys to enjoy the river. It's my pleasure, really. My grandpa used to say, 'Stay low, John. Stay low. This whole thing ain't about you. Disappear into the river. The joy in life is in thinking about others more than yourself.' My job is to serve you, period. Let's eat!"

1. Name three people in your life you believe to be truly humble. Describe why you feel this way about them.

_____

_____

_____

_____

_____

_____

2. Has there ever been a time in your life when you realized that pride had taken root in your heart?

_____

_____

_____

_____

3. What are tangible, specific ways to combat pride in our lives?

_____

_____

_____

_____

4. Is there a job you feel is beneath you? If so, what is it and why?

_____

_____

_____

_____

METAPHOR

Do nothing out of selfish ambition or vain conceit. Rather, in humility value others above yourselves, not looking to your own interests but each of you to the interests of the others.

—PHILIPPIANS 2:3–4

1. Name a biblical character you feel embodies humility. Why?

_____

_____

_____

2. Name a biblical character you feel embodies pride. Why?

_____

_____

_____

3. Name five ways you can actively value others above yourself.

_____

_____

_____

_____

_____

4. How will pride ruin your ability to hear the Lord?

_____

_____

_____

_____

_____

5. How will pride affect your ability to lead others?

_____

_____

_____

_____

_____

WISDOM

1. What does humility look like in a person's life?

_____

_____

_____

_____

2. What does humility look like in a worshiper? Be specific.

_____

_____

_____

_____

3. The foundational qualifications for the Spirit-filled worship leader begins with the ability to demonstrate a genuine, humble, servant-leadership attitude. Why does this kind of posture require a life of surrender? What are the benefits and blessings of such an attitude?

_____

_____

_____

_____

4. In your opinion, how does humility help you to be obedient?

_____

_____

_____

_____

5. Why do you think humility requires trust in God? Being really honest with yourself . . . articulate the areas of your life where God needs to help you eliminate a prideful or haughty spirit.

_____

_____

_____

_____

CHAPTER 13

INTEGRITY

Who you are: Living out your character honestly before God and others.

STORY

"Apparently, the guide from that raft put his rafters in jeopardy. He was with another company. Word is he had a shoulder injury or something that may have prevented him from steering properly and when the kid fell out, he didn't follow protocol. Who knows if that guide actually coached him well or if he just panicked. It sounds like once the boy fell in, he fought the whitewater instead of letting it take him. He tried to climb up on a rock over and over until he exhausted himself and he just got pinned in the keeper."

"What's a keeper?" I asked.

"The water pours down into a large crevice in the riverbed and within the giant wave it folds back on itself and just keeps churning. It keeps anything that falls into it. Hence, keeper."

"Man, I wouldn't want to be that guide," I commented. "The guilt alone would be crushing."

"Yeah, it's one thing when an accident happens. It's a whole other thing when you present yourself as healthy and ready to roll and you aren't. He has probably disqualified himself from guiding commercially. At any rate, I've rafted this rapid hundreds of times and never had an issue. We'll be fine!"

1. Define integrity in your own words.

_____

_____

_____

_____

2. How did the guide in the story compromise his integrity?

_____

_____

_____

_____

3. Why is integrity important?

_____

_____

_____

_____

4. How does integrity affect your role as a worshiper?

_____

_____

_____

_____

5. As a leader?

_____

_____

_____

6. As a friend?

_____

_____

_____

7. As a spouse?

_____
_____
_____
_____
_____
_____

8. As a parent?

_____
_____
_____
_____
_____
_____

9. Picture your life as a house. If Jesus is the cornerstone, what part of the house would integrity be?

_____
_____
_____
_____
_____
_____
_____

METAPHOR

The integrity of the upright guides them,
but the unfaithful are destroyed by their duplicity.
—PROVERBS 11:3

1. List three characters in Scripture who lacked integrity. How did they show this, and what were the consequences?

_____
_____
_____
_____
_____
_____

2. List three characters who God used powerfully, but they compromised their integrity. Again, write down how you recognized this, and what the consequences were.

_____

_____

_____

_____

_____

3. List seven ways, by the power of the Holy Spirit, you can fortify your integrity.

_____

_____

_____

_____

_____

_____

WISDOM

1. Why is integrity important for the worship leader?

_____

_____

_____

_____

_____

2. Character, brokenness, humility, ethics, morality, and integrity are pillars that support the life given to worship. After studying this chapter on integrity, fill in the blanks below:

    a. **Character** refers to _____.

    b. **Brokenness** refers to _____.

    c. **Humility** is _____.

    d. **Ethics** refers to _____.

    e. **Morality** is _____.

    f. **Integrity** refers to _____.

3. How is integrity different from character?

_____

_____

_____

_____

4. In what ways is integrity (or lack of it) reflected in how worship leaders carry out their various tasks and roles?

_____

_____

_____

_____

5. Have you ever been tempted to be dishonest instead of protecting your integrity? How do you fight that temptation?

_____

_____

_____

_____

6. In what way does our skill in leading worship reflect our commitment to a life of praise, integrity, and obedience? Explain.

_____

_____

_____

_____

CHAPTER 14

LIVING WATER

The water I give will become a spring of water gushing
up inside that person, giving eternal life.

STORY

"There was a time a few years ago when I wanted out of the family business.
My dad and I had it out, so I took off. I was exploring, traveling, getting into
some bad stuff. I was searching for the meaning of it all, I guess. I ended
up pretty bankrupt, in every way, not just financially. My search brought me
nothing but heartache. The short version of it is, I came back. My dad is
incredible. He welcomed me back. This time I actually surrendered to him
and to my destiny with the river. That's when I got serious about becoming
one with the river, and everything settled for me. I was finally at rest. I was
satisfied, no longer aching for something else to bring me joy and purpose.
I didn't need to chase anything else. It's all found in the river for me."

* * *

"So, does that mean you never leave and do other things?"

"No, not at all. It means the river never leaves me. See, I raft rivers all
over the world. I travel and explore. It just means I'm satisfied. I don't need
to chase other things . . . money, relationships, power, influence. I'm good.
I'm just good."

1. Think of a time you have found yourself trying to satisfy your longings in things besides Jesus. What were those things?

_____

_____

_____

_____

2. How did God meet you and bring you back?

_____

_____

_____

_____

3. Why are we "prone to wander"?

_____

_____

_____

_____

4. How does the enemy try to shape our thirst for things other than God?

_____

_____

_____

_____

5. How long can a human go without water?

_____

_____

_____

_____

6. Find five Scripture passages—either Old or New Testament—where rivers or water are used. Note them here.

_____

_____

_____

_____

7. In each instance, what does water represent?

_____

_____

_____

_____

METAPHOR

Jesus answered, "Everyone who drinks this water will be thirsty again, but whoever drinks the water I give them will never thirst. Indeed, the water I give them will become in them a spring of water welling up to eternal life." The woman said to him, "Sir, give me this water so that I won't get thirsty and have to keep coming here to draw water."

—JOHN 4:13–15

1. List as many things as you can that we tend to chase to satisfy our thirst in life.

_____

_____

_____

_____

_____

_____

_____

_____

2. How do these things affect our worship of Jesus? Be specific.

_____

_____

_____

3. How does idolatry play a role here?

_____

_____

_____

4. Many times, we can be operating in ministry but actually thirsting for the wrong things. How does that look practically?

_____

_____

_____

_____

5. Describe three ways you are able to keep your thirst for God, his presence, and his Word.

_____

_____

_____

_____

WISDOM

1. Describe what spiritual thirst looks like in your life.

_____

_____

_____

_____

2. What do you think Jesus was referring to when he spoke of "living water"?

_____

_____

_____

_____

3. When Jesus tells the Samaritan woman, "Whoever drinks of this water will thirst again" (John 4:13 NKJV), he is seeking to meet a deeply personal, spiritual need in the woman's heart. What spiritual thirst is that? In what ways is Jesus seeking to satisfy your own personal spiritual thirst?

_____

_____

_____

4. In what three ways does the "living water" encounter in John 4:11 apply to those seeking The Way of Worship?

     a. Jesus is the S_____ of Living Water.
     b. Jesus creates in us S_____ of Living Water.
     c. Jesus provides S_____ in this Living Water.

5. Jesus is the source for fresh, daily renewable worship that ever bubbles up to overflowing with blessing and spiritual nourishment. In your opinion, how does this happen?

_____

_____

_____

_____

C. HIS POWER, OUR AWARENESS

CHAPTER 15

GENEROSITY

From an overflow of abundance, we give with every type of resource.

STORY

"The river is always giving you something new, something fresh. I never get tired of it. Look at the beautiful trees, the flowers, the wildlife, it just keeps giving."

John chimed in. "Totally. The river brings life. Water is the source, man. It has given me everything, why would I hold anything back? You can't out give the river."

John possessed a generous spirit. He seemed bound only by the responsibility he felt to serve others. You got this sense from him during the whole trip that he would give you the shirt off his back if needed. He had great ownership of his role, but he was not owned by it, or anything for that matter. He was free.

1. In your life, list three people who have been extremely generous to you. Describe how they were generous. (time, encouragement, money, etc.)

_____

_____

_____

_____

_____

2. Now describe a situation where someone was stingy or tight-fisted with you. Again, think beyond just money.

_____

_____

_____

_____

_____

3. How does generosity correlate to and deepen our worship of God?

_____

_____

_____

_____

_____

_____

4. In a few sentences, describe a generous way of living, as if you had every resource at your fingertips.

_____

_____

_____

_____

_____

_____

_____

METAPHOR

Give, and it will be given to you. A good measure, pressed down, shaken together and running over, will be poured into your lap. For with the measure you use, it will be measured to you.

—LUKE 6:38

1. Note a passage of Scripture where you see the generosity of God, practically.

_____

_____

_____

_____

2. What was the result of God's generosity in that passage?

_____
_____
_____
_____

3. List three passages of Scripture where you see human generosity. Be specific in describing what effect this had.

_____
_____
_____
_____
_____
_____
_____

4. List seven ways you can manifest generosity to your ministry partners or the teams you lead.

_____
_____
_____
_____
_____
_____
_____
_____
_____

WISDOM

1. It's easy to imagine how generosity to other people helps them, but what does it mean to be generous with the Lord?

_____
_____
_____

2. How does generosity affect our character? Our worship?

_____

_____

_____

_____

3. How does understanding what Christ has done for us encourage us to be generous?

_____

_____

_____

_____

4. James 1:17 says, "Every good and perfect gift is from above." What "good and perfect gifts" has God given you?

_____

_____

_____

_____

5. According to Psalm 96:7-8, a person who is faithful to worship in spirit and truth naturally demonstrates adoration to the Lord with a generous and unselfish spirit in three ways. Fill in the following in explaining the three ways a person demonstrates a giving spirit:

   a. Give to the L_____ glory. (v. 7)
   b. Give to the Lord s_____. (v. 7)
   c. Give to the Lord an o_____. (v. 8)

6. What are the four types of biblical gifts?

   a. Gifts of H_____.
   b. Gifts of H_____.
   c. H_____ Gifts.
   d. H_____ Gifts.

7. In what ways might God be asking you to be more generous in your life right now?

_____

_____

_____

CHAPTER 16

EQUIPPING

Accept the training of those who went before you,
and support and teach those who come after.

STORY

"I take courses in water safety, first aid, and hydrology. I take guide training courses. I meet with apprentice guides weekly. We have certifications and tests we have to go through. We also have a briefing before every trip. We actually met for an hour before you came in this morning. We will meet after to evaluate how it went and what we can learn. We are constantly learning. The more you know, the more confident you become. John always says, 'It's the way of the guide.'

"I found whatever nerves I had were waning and my comfort grew in knowing the lengths to which these guides go to stay ready, equipping themselves and each other for the great privilege and responsibility of guiding."

1. Describe a situation you felt ill-equipped to handle.

_____

_____

_____

_____

_____

2. How did that affect you? How did it affect others?

_____

_____

_____

_____

3. Was there something you could've done to be more prepared?

_____

_____

_____

_____

4. In your area of ministry, list five specific ways you need to be equipped. (It could be training, resources, etc.)

_____

_____

_____

_____

5. To equip and be equipped requires trust in both directions. Describe someone you **trust** to equip you and why.

_____

_____

_____

_____

_____

METAPHOR

And He Himself gave some to be apostles, some prophets, some evangelists, and some pastors and teachers, for the equipping of the saints for the work of ministry, for the edifying of the body of Christ, till we all come to the unity of the faith and of the knowledge of the Son of God, to a perfect man, to the measure of the stature of the fullness of Christ.
—EPHESIANS 4:11–13 NKJV

1. Who has God put in your life to equip you with knowledge and experience?

_____
_____
_____
_____
_____
_____

2. What opportunities has God given you to equip others? In what specific ways can you help them?

_____
_____
_____
_____
_____
_____

3. When leading a team, how does the equipping process bring unity?

_____
_____
_____
_____
_____
_____

4. In what ways does equipping others equip you?

_____
_____
_____
_____
_____

5. What character traits must you have to both be equipped and to equip others? (e.g., humility, tenacity, etc.) Give a reason for each trait.

_____
_____
_____
_____
_____

WISDOM

1. In your opinion, how does the command to go into all the world apply to you?

_____

_____

_____

2. What is the difference between being a teacher and an equipper?

_____

_____

_____

3. In what ways does this kind of equipping drill down to the core of one's being?

_____

_____

_____

_____

4. How have you seen the Holy Spirit equip you with "everything good and appropriate for doing his will"?

_____

_____

_____

_____

5. How can worship leaders become better equipped for their task?

_____

_____

_____

_____

6. How do you think worship leaders build their confidence each time they equip people for works of service?

_____

_____

_____

CHAPTER 17

EMPOWERING

Allow others to guide and release the apprentices
to lead, and then become a good follower.

STORY

"The sidewinder is all you, Ana!"

Ana looked bewildered.

"You know what to do," John said encouragingly. "Let's switch. You take the command on this rapid."

John and Anastasia gripped forearms as they stood and swapped places. John moved to the port side rear and Ana moved to the guide's perch at the center on the back tube.

"Everyone, please take your commands from the Swede on this next rapid. It's a tricky one . . . very technical."

He did not coddle, nor did he demean. I was a first timer, but his forthrightness gave me a level of confidence in his ability, Ana's ability, and my own. I never felt the sense that he was instructing from a need for power or authority, only service and purpose. His presence and manner were impressive in all the right ways . . .

We careened over the next rapid in reverse and then John, straining and digging deep into the water with his paddle, quickly spun us around after we navigated safely.

"I'm sorry, I'm sorry. I missed that call." Ana looked dejected.

"We made it and avoided an unnecessary brisk swim, thankfully."

"It happened so quickly, I just missed it."

"It's okay, you learned what not to do next time. That's why I'm here. It happens. Move forward. You can do this."

1. Has there ever been a time when you have been given a task to do but were not empowered to do it? If so, describe that circumstance.

_____

_____

_____

_____

_____

2. What are some consequences in our local churches if we do not empower others to fulfill their calling and do the ministry of the church?

_____

_____

_____

_____

_____

3. Name five things a person needs in order to empower others, each with a qualifying statement. (e.g., An empowering person is secure. They know who they are and are not threatened by another person's strength.)

_____

_____

_____

_____

_____

_____

_____

_____

4. Choose a narrative in Scripture where a leader empowered someone else to lead. Note the Scripture reference and describe the scenario in your own words.

_____

_____

_____

METAPHOR

Command and teach these things. Don't let anyone look down on you because you are young, but set an example for the believers in speech, in conduct, in love, in faith, in purity. Until I come, devote yourself to the public reading of Scripture, to preaching and to teaching. Do not neglect your gift, which was given you through prophecy when the body of elders laid their hands on you.

—1 TIMOTHY 4:11–14

1. We use the term "supported empowerment." What does that mean to you?

_____

_____

_____

2. Why is it important to empower others at the appropriate time and with the appropriate equipping?

_____

_____

_____

3. What happens if someone is given too much power too soon?

_____

_____

_____

WISDOM

1. What is the relationship between and/or difference between being equipped and being empowered?

_____

_____

_____

_____

2. How do you think worshipers, as disciples of the Lord Jesus Christ, are equipped with spiritual strength? (Check out Luke 9:1–6.)

_____

_____

_____

3. After reading Exodus 35:30–35, list the skill-set with which God gifts and empowers Betzalel:

   a. Design _____.
   b. Work in _____.
   c. Cut _____.
   d. Carving _____.
   e. Create cloth, make _____.
   f. Function as a _____.
   g. Do all manner of _____.

4. How does God empower his people? Explain.

_____

_____

_____

5. List the ways you believe God has uniquely gifted you and wants you to use your gifts and skill-set for the purpose of advancing his kingdom. Explain in one or two sentences.

_____

_____

_____

_____

_____

_____

_____

6. What does it mean that God obligates himself to equip and empower the worshiper? How should it impact our actions and attitude?

_____

_____

_____

CHAPTER 18

UNIFYING

Unite rafters (leaders, musicians, artists) to paddle in unison, in the same direction, and to always be looking out for one another.

STORY

"When you paddle, you gotta mean it. It's important that we all dig in and execute powerfully together. If I give a 'forward hard' command and one side doesn't dig in, what do you think happens?"

"We spin?" I replied quickly.

"Yes, and if we spin and head sideways into a deep rapid or some falls what happens?"

"We swim," Leah replied.

"Exactly. We spin, we swim. Unity is everything, so let's work together so that everyone experiences something spectacular."

In life you are either preparing or repairing.

—JOHN C. MAXWELL

1. In what ways can you prepare the people you lead to be unified?

_____

_____

_____

_____

2. Describe an instance when you have seen disunity or division. What were the consequences?

_____

_____

_____

_____

3. Even if people aren't malicious, division can take hold. What must you do as a leader to keep people paddling in the right direction? (e.g., communicate the vision, etc.)

_____

_____

_____

_____

METAPHOR

How good and pleasant it is
 when God's people live together in unity!
It is like precious oil poured on the head,
 running down on the beard,
running down on Aaron's beard,
 down on the collar of his robe.
It is as if the dew of Hermon
 were falling on Mount Zion.
For there the Lord bestows his blessing,
 even life forevermore.
      —PSALM 133

1. Think of an orchestra. List three or more things an instrumentalist must do to promote unity in the orchestra.

_____

_____

_____

_____

2. How about the conductor?

_____

_____

_____

_____

_____

_____

3. People and organizations don't drift toward unity. It takes great intentionality. List five ways you can practically help a ministry team stay unified.

_____

_____

_____

_____

_____

_____

_____

_____

4. Consider the Trinity—the triune God. Describe how the Father, Son, and Holy Spirit are unified.

_____

_____

_____

_____

_____

5. How does unity honor God?

_____

_____

_____

_____

6. Unity is essential in the way of worship. Can you describe why? Use Scripture.

_____

_____

_____

_____

WISDOM

1. A unifying spirit cannot be demonstrated without the worshiper's commitment to what three areas?

_____

_____

_____

_____

_____

2. What are the evidences of a spirit of unity?

_____

_____

_____

_____

_____

3. Why would you think the entire praise team or worship ministry is at their strongest when they are one in heart, mind, and purpose?

_____

_____

_____

_____

_____

4. There are four strategic ingredients for the creation of a unified team: Unity of Mind, Unity of Heart, Unity of Love, and Unity of Spirit. In your own words, write a sentence describing how each one of these areas is strategic for the worship:

    a. Unity of Mind

_____

_____

_____

_____

b. Unity of Heart

_____

_____

_____

_____

_____

c. Unity of Love

_____

_____

_____

_____

_____

d. Unity of Spirit

_____

_____

_____

_____

_____

5. What do you think it looks like for lowliness, forbearance, gentleness, and longsuffering to characterize someone's life?

_____

_____

_____

_____

CHAPTER 19

SERVING

Others before self.

STORY

"Take it easy," John said to the loopy rafter as he loosened his life vest.

The young man leaned over and vomited violently all over John.

"Whoa, whoa buddy." John helped him lean over and finish heaving without spraying anyone. "Looks like you got yourself a concussion."

John proceeded to get a towel from his dry bag and wipe the young man off. He got him some fresh water to drink and then splashed river water on his soiled shirt and life vest.

"What's your name?" John asked him.

"Tommy . . . really sorry about getting sick on you. I just got really dizzy."

"Don't sweat it, bud. Take some deep breaths. We are going to get medics out here to take you in and get you evaluated. You'll be all right, but by the looks of that helmet you rocked your noggin good."

1. Describe a time when you did something for someone who couldn't do anything for you in return.

_____

_____

_____

_____

2. How did that make you feel?

_____

_____

_____

_____

3. Show in Scripture how that act correlated to worship?

_____

_____

_____

_____

4. In Scripture, point out a narrative of someone (other than Jesus) that depicts the power of serving.

_____

_____

_____

_____

5. In our story, we see serving someone can be messy. Describe a time when you or someone you know served someone and it got you messy.

_____

_____

_____

_____

_____

METAPHOR

In your relationships with one another, have the same mindset as Christ Jesus: Who, being in very nature God, did not consider equality with God something to be used to his own advantage; rather, he made himself nothing by taking the very nature of a servant, being made in human likeness. And being found in appearance as a man, he humbled himself by becoming obedient to death—even death on a cross!

—PHILIPPIANS 2:5–8

1. What are some practical ways you can serve your fellow teammates in ministry?

_____

_____

_____

_____

2. What are some practical ways you can serve "the least of these"? (the poor, weak, sick, disabled, etc.)

_____

_____

_____

_____

3. How often do you believe we should schedule intentional service of others?

_____

_____

_____

_____

4. What are some ways we can serve anonymously?

_____

_____

_____

_____

5. How does this fuel and inform our worship?

_____

_____

_____

_____

6. What are the personal and tangible benefits we actually receive from serving others?

_____

_____

_____

_____

WISDOM

1. How does the culture around you encourage you to seek your own ambition instead of humility and a servant attitude?

_____

_____

_____

_____

2. Why do you think worshipers need to guard against self-ambition, self-reliance, and self-determination?

_____

_____

_____

_____

3. What does the chapter on "serving" mean when it describes "vertical" and "horizontal" relationships? How do they affect one another?

_____

_____

_____

_____

4. How did Jesus demonstrate servant leadership?

_____

_____

_____

_____

5. According to Romans 12:2, 10 and 15:9, worshipers should be "transformed by the renewing of their mind." How does this "transformation principle" enable a worshiper to be devoted to one another in brotherly love?

_____

_____

_____

6. In our study on "serving," the author gives a list of ten areas in which the worshiper can demonstrate a servant attitude. List five of those principles below:

a. S_____.

b. S_____.

c. S_____.

d. S_____.

e. S_____.

CHAPTER 20

SACRIFICING

Willing to lay down your life for the mission.

STORY

"He is so passionate about the river," John said. "He really wanted to care for this land. He wanted something to pass down to the generations behind him. Nearly everything you see around here he built with his own hands. His mission is to help as many people as possible fall in love with the river."

"So, is that your mission too?" I asked.

"Yeah, you could say that. When you find something so amazing, you want others to experience it too. Whatever you have to give up, to live that purpose out, it's no sacrifice at all really, it's just joy . . . all joy."

"So, you've given some stuff up then?"

"Just stuff." John replied with a grin. "It's a lot . . . you know to take care of this place, to manage the business and to prepare yourself for the river physically and mentally. It definitely costs you. It's a price worth paying though. You'll see."

1. Think of a time in your life when you had to give up something to gain a greater thing. What did you have to give up?

_____

_____

_____

2. Did you regret it? Explain.

_____

_____

_____

_____

_____

3. Name three historical figures (extra-biblical) who sacrificed for the greater good.

_____

_____

_____

_____

_____

4. Describe the impact of their lives.

_____

_____

_____

_____

_____

5. Name a scriptural passage where someone was not willing to sacrifice for the greater thing.

_____

_____

_____

_____

_____

6. Describe where that decision left them.

_____

_____

_____

_____

7. Why does worship have to cost us something?

_____

_____

_____

_____

METAPHOR

But the king replied to Araunah, "No, I insist on paying you for it. I will not sacrifice to the LORD my God burnt offerings that cost me nothing." So David bought the threshing floor and the oxen and paid fifty shekels of silver for them. David built an altar to the LORD there and sacrificed burnt offerings and fellowship offerings. Then the LORD answered his prayer in behalf of the land, and the plague on Israel was stopped.

—2 SAMUEL 24:24–25

1. What kinds of sacrifices do you think it takes to lead teams in ministry? (Think time, relational energy, resource, etc.)

_____

_____

_____

_____

_____

2. Since God no longer requires a blood sacrifice to enter his presence, what does a sacrifice of praise really mean?

_____

_____

_____

_____

_____

_____

3. What are five practical ways you can model costly sacrifice in your own life and ministry?

_____

_____

_____

_____

_____

_____

4. We all have carnal desires we need to lay on the altar of sacrifice. What are they for you? (e.g., pride, achievement, etc.)

_____

_____

_____

_____

WISDOM

1. What kind of sacrifice does God require of worshipers today? And what does it mean to be a "living sacrifice" to the Lord?

_____

_____

_____

2. Why are the Old Testament practices of killing animals for the atonement of sin no longer needed?

_____

_____

_____

3. Why, if Jesus has once and for all done away with the "sacrifice," does the epistle to the Hebrews urge, if not require, New Testament believers to "offer to God our sacrifice of praise"?

_____

_____

_____

_____

4. Why is it important that, when we give, we expect nothing in return?

_____

_____

_____

5. What does it mean to guard your heart?

_____

_____

_____

_____

6. In your opinion, what is meant by:

   a. Sacrifice of Thanksgiving

   _____

   _____

   _____

   _____

   b. Sacrifice of Righteousness

   _____

   _____

   _____

   _____

   c. Sacrifice of our Prayer

   _____

   _____

   _____

   _____

   d. Sacrifice of Peace

   _____

   _____

   _____

CHAPTER 21

CRAFT

Excellence honors God, inspires others, and removes distraction.

STORY

"John, so how long did it take you to become a guide?"

"Well, it didn't take too long to learn the basics and become certified at the lowest levels. I had a head start with being around it so much with my father." He paused. "There's a big difference in initially getting certified and being a master guide, though. I guess we're kind of like doctors. There are doctors who just get a medical degree, and then there are doctors you'll trust your life with . . . You got to stay humble and hungry if you really want to experience the good stuff safely. I see some of these other yahoos taking other people down the river who have no business guiding. They don't take it seriously. It never ends well. Those who chase it . . . those are the ones that really honor the river and those they guide. It's the only way."

"Chase what?" I asked.

He smiled wildly with his hand draped over the steering wheel.

"The very best version of everything."

1. Think of a concert or performance that was so excellent that it transported you.

_____

_____

_____

2. Describe why it was so incredible. Be specific.

_____
_____
_____
_____
_____

3. Imagine what an orchestra's journey involved to become so great.

_____
_____
_____
_____
_____

4. Describe a piece of fine art that you love.

_____
_____
_____
_____

5. Who created it?

_____
_____
_____
_____

6. How did the painter or sculptor become great?

_____
_____
_____
_____

7. Have you ever visited a cathedral or house of worship that moved you by its architecture? If so, name it and who designed it, if possible. Describe what makes it so beautiful.

_____
_____
_____
_____

METAPHOR

The workers labored faithfully. Over them to direct them were Jahath and Obadiah, Levites descended from Merari, and Zechariah and Meshullam, descended from Kohath. The Levites—all who were skilled in playing musical instruments—had charge of the laborers and supervised all the workers from job to job. Some of the Levites were secretaries, scribes and gatekeepers.
—2 CHRONICLES 34:12–13

1. Name your primary areas of ministry. (worship leader, singer, guitar player, team coordinator, administrative assistant, etc.)

_____

_____

_____

2. Rank these areas in order of your ability. Start at the top with your greatest competency.

_____

_____

_____

3. Do you spend a lot of time doing things you are not good at? If so, explain.

_____

_____

_____

_____

4. For your top two areas of gifting, list five ways in which you can improve your skill.

_____

_____

_____

_____

_____

_____

_____

_____

5. Describe how honing your craft strengthens your worship life.

_____

_____

_____

_____

6. Specifically, why is it so important to pursue the very best version of your craft?

_____

_____

_____

_____

WISDOM

1. How does seeing worship as our calling affect the way we develop and steward our craft?

_____

_____

_____

_____

_____

2. What is required to pursue your craft well?

_____

_____

_____

_____

_____

3. What gifts do you think God has given you to steward? Explain how this stewarding is accomplished.

_____

_____

_____

_____

_____

4. Why is competence important for a worship leader?

_____

_____

_____

_____

5. What is the difference between craft and competence? Explain.

_____

_____

_____

_____

D. HIS WORK, OUR RELATIONSHIPS

CHAPTER 22

COMMUNICATION

Be clear in your directives, your plan, and your purpose.

STORY

"Okay, guys, circle up here before we head back out. I've got some info for you on this next rapid. You're going to want to pay attention," John said as he motioned us over.

We were finishing the last bites of our lunch at a pebbled beach by the river.

"I wasn't sure I wanted to tell you guys this because I didn't want to freak you out."

Leah and I quickly caught each other's eye. He certainly had our attention now.

"This next rapid is not a problem if you pay attention and we hit it right," he said. "If not, bad things can happen. Yesterday, a twenty-one-year-old guy died in this rapid."

My heart sank. We were all stunned.

"We must go in fast and straight on. If you follow my commands, we won't have any issue. I haven't had any swimmers here, so don't worry. I just need to make sure you hear me and follow me. It's a really fun and exciting rapid!"

1. Describe a time when, under supervision, you did something potentially dangerous.

_____
_____
_____
_____
_____

2. Did the supervising person give you good instructions about what to expect? If yes, how did that make you feel? More safe and confident? If no, how did that make you feel? Confused? Scared?

_____
_____
_____
_____
_____

3. Describe a narrative in Scripture where the main character communicated effectively.

_____
_____
_____
_____
_____

4. What was a result of the effective communication?

_____
_____
_____
_____

5. Now do the same where the opposite happened.

_____
_____
_____
_____
_____

METAPHOR

The tongue of the wise commends knowledge,
but the mouths of fools pour out folly.
—PROVERBS 15:2 ESV

1. List five distinguishing characteristics of good communication.

_____
_____
_____
_____
_____
_____

2. List five reasons good communication is necessary for leadership.

_____
_____
_____
_____
_____
_____

3. List five results of having a leader who communicates poorly.

_____
_____
_____
_____
_____
_____

4. Describe a situation when it might take great courage to communicate effectively.

_____
_____
_____
_____

5. Why would you need courage?

6. What happens when there is a gap or void in our communication with those we are in ministry with or leading?

WISDOM

1. How does communication affect areas such as relationships, team building, congregational/group worship, stewardship, submission, obedience, character, and trust?

2. What is the difference between temperament and testimony?

3. In your opinion, what does it mean for a worshiper to practice humble communication?

4. What are some characteristics of harmful and healthy communication? What are the results, and how does harmful communication defile the worshiper?

_____

_____

_____

_____

_____

_____

_____

5. What is one way you are developing and practicing healthy communication this week?

_____

_____

_____

_____

6. How can the worshiper guard against developing a critical spirit?

_____

_____

_____

_____

7. How can you recognize when your communication has become critical toward others?

_____

_____

_____

_____

8. How do you think a worshiper can practice honesty and confidence (not arrogance), listen carefully, reflect on and respect other's opinions, be open and friendly, speak softly, and demonstrate healthy communication?

_____

_____

_____

_____

CHAPTER 23

CONFIDENCE

Knowing who and whose you are, and that you are
destined to lead. You must be confident in your calling,
knowing where your humble strength comes from.

STORY

"I haven't always been confident," John said as he walked past us.

I followed him. "So where . . . when did you find it?"

He kept moving. "I think confidence comes from knowing who you are and what you put your confidence in."

I needed more.

"So, what does that mean for you?" I questioned again.

"I was made for the river, plain and simple. Once I embraced that, the outside couldn't tell me who I was. I'm anchored. It keeps things clear for me. For a while I tried to let circumstances or people define me. Not anymore. True confidence comes from knowing who you are . . .

"If you don't know who you are, you'll spend your whole life chasing someone else's idea of who you should be. That's a surefire way into the arms of fear. Once you sort out your identity, you find your confidence, plain and simple."

1. Would you describe yourself as naturally confident?

_____

_____

2. If yes, explain why you are a confident person. If no, explain why you feel you lack confidence.

_____

_____

_____

_____

3. Name three famous characters in the Bible who lacked confidence, yet God used them mightily. Include a sentence of why each didn't feel fit for their mission.

_____

_____

_____

_____

_____

4. Note as many differences as you can between arrogance and confidence.

_____

_____

_____

_____

METAPHOR

The LORD is my light and my salvation—
   whom shall I fear?
The LORD is the stronghold of my life—
   of whom shall I be afraid?
When the wicked advance against me
   to devour me,
it is my enemies and my foes
   who will stumble and fall.

Though an army besiege me,
my heart will not fear;
though war break out against me,
even then I will be confident.
—PSALM 27:1–3

1. Think of some things that cause you to fear.

_____

_____

_____

_____

2. What do you think God wants you to know in the midst of that fear? Point to passages in Scripture that speak to this.

_____

_____

_____

_____

3. What are some things that can cause you to lose confidence in your calling?

_____

_____

_____

_____

_____

4. What do the promises of God say about those things?

_____

_____

_____

_____

5. List five ways to build your confidence in the Lord.

_____

_____

_____

_____

6. List five ways to help someone else build their confidence in the Lord.

_____
_____
_____
_____
_____
_____

WISDOM

1. In your opinion, what does it mean for God to be our confidence? What does confidence look like, practically, in the life of a worshiper?

_____
_____
_____
_____

2. There is strength when the worshiper's confidence comes from the Lord. What three basic resources does God provide with his strength?

        a. P_____
        b. P_____
        c. P_____

3. Have you ever "lost heart"? What does it look like? How can we guard against it?

_____
_____
_____
_____

4. Why is the worshiper's confidence not found in a stronger self-image or self-assurance? How is godly confidence different from earthly confidence?

_____
_____
_____
_____

5. Once worshipers, and those leading worship, discover and understand that their true confidence is only found in Jesus, they can be assured that (fill in the blanks using *The Way of Worship* book [pp. 225–232] or video):

    a. He willingly hears our _____ and _____.

    b. He joyfully joins us _____ we _____.

    c. He graciously serves as our _____ high _____.

    d. He forever _____ his _____.

    e. He gives power to those that _____ him . . .

    f. He renews _____ every _____.

    g. He ever _____—on our behalf.

    h. He serves as our own, _____ worship _____.

    i. He genuinely protects and _____ against the forces of _____.

    j. He teaches you and me _____ to lead _____!

Now this is the **confidence** that we have in Him, that if we ask anything according to His will, He hears us.

    —1 JOHN 5:14 NKJV

CHAPTER 24

NAVIGATION

We help people shift their highest affections from themselves
and ascribe ultimate worth to Jesus. We are gospel pointers.

STORY

"Absolutely. It's how I navigate. You have to plan. You have to chart your course. You have to pay attention to what the river is saying. The guides share information from day to day, we scout early in the morning, we make our plan and then we execute. You know what Ben Franklin said, right?"

"I'm not sure, what?"

"'By failing to prepare, you are preparing to fail.'" That's strong, isn't it? The reality is, sometimes you have to make last-minute adjustments. You can't mitigate all risk, but if you have a foundational preparation, you will navigate well. The stakes are too high not to.

1. How would you plan a road trip without GPS or Google Maps to guide you?

_____

_____

_____

_____

_____

_____

2. Who would you/should you involve?

_____

_____

_____

_____

3. What tools would you need?

_____

_____

_____

_____

4. In the same fashion, how could you chart your course for your life?

_____

_____

_____

_____

5. What tools would you need?

_____

_____

_____

_____

6. Who would you/should you involve in the decisions?

_____

_____

_____

_____

7. At its core, navigation is about intentionality. How are you being intentional about charting a course for the following areas of your life? Name three small steps for each that you can focus on for the next six months:

Your physical health

_____

_____

_____

Your financial stewardship

_____

_____

_____

_____

Your relationships

_____

_____

_____

_____

Your spiritual health

_____

_____

_____

_____

Your career path

_____

_____

_____

_____

_____

METAPHOR

You are my portion, Lord;
    I have promised to obey your words.
I have sought your face with all my heart;
    be gracious to me according to your promise.
I have considered my ways
    and have turned my steps to your statutes.
I will hasten and not delay
    to obey your commands.
            —PSALM 119:57–60

1. What are some practical ways you can lead a ministry team on a steady course? You can use the categories listed above.

_____

_____

_____

_____

_____

2. In this chapter we speak of being "gospel pointers." How can you practically point people to the gospel?

_____

_____

_____

_____

_____

3. What role can the arts play in helping people navigate? Be specific.

_____

_____

_____

_____

_____

4. List four practical ways we can make sure our navigation plans aren't leading us off course.

_____

_____

_____

_____

_____

5. List at least three narratives in Scripture where God equips the people with clear plans.

_____

_____

_____

_____

_____

WISDOM

1. What is King Solomon's formula for being successful in life (Proverbs 3:5–6), and how does trusting the Lord affect how you lead others?

_____

_____

_____

_____

2. How does God's sovereignty help us navigate the challenges worshipers are facing every day?

_____

_____

_____

_____

3. What does it look like to trust God's plan for your life, rather than your own? And, what does it mean to trust his process?

_____

_____

_____

_____

4. In what ways do you believe God desires to use you to fulfill his purposes?

_____

_____

_____

_____

5. In what ways are fulfilling God's purpose and calling a process?

_____

_____

_____

_____

CHAPTER 25

VISION

Seeing where the waters are moving and speaking of what
is to come is key to guiding well. Be prophetic.

STORY

"When I take people down the river, I really want them to see what I see, and know what I know."

John had a way of communicating almost cryptically, forcing you to engage and ask more questions. He wouldn't just come out with it. He drew you in. It was frustrating and intriguing at the same time. It was certainly memorable.

"You want us to see the river differently or something?" I asked.

"I want you to see what's beyond the river. If you're awake to it, you won't be the same."

I was growing more impatient.

"Now I just feel dumb. What is it you want us to see?"

"In this moment, what are the most important things to you?" John asked.

I thought for a moment. "Leah, of course. My faith. My family."

"Beautiful," he said. "If you're anything like me, being out here, being in the river, has purified what is most important to you. Being in the river to me means not allowing my passions to be consumed by lesser things. My hope is people will go back to their everyday lives with a renewed sense of the proper order of things. A renewed resolve that they are chasing the right things. Not money, comfort, or notoriety, but something far greater. Faith, hope, and love. Generously giving themselves away to care, lift up, and heal."

1. Think of a time when someone helped you see something about yourself or your life that you couldn't recognize on your own.

_____

_____

_____

_____

_____

2. How did that help you?

_____

_____

_____

_____

_____

3. Describe a time when you were focused on the things that weren't the most important.

_____

_____

_____

_____

_____

4. Do you have a vision for your life personally? If so, describe it.

_____

_____

_____

_____

_____

5. List five ways you can equip yourself to see things clearly in the way of worship.

_____

_____

_____

_____

_____

METAPHOR

The Spirit of the Sovereign Lord is on me,
      because the Lord has anointed me
      to proclaim good news to the poor.
He has sent me to bind up the brokenhearted,
      to proclaim freedom for the captives
      and release from darkness for the prisoners,
to proclaim the year of the Lord's favor
      and the day of vengeance of our God,
to comfort all who mourn,
      and provide for those who grieve in Zion—
to bestow on them a crown of beauty
      instead of ashes,
the oil of joy
      instead of mourning,
and a garment of praise
      instead of a spirit of despair.
They will be called oaks of righteousness,
      a planting of the Lord
      for the display of his splendor.
                              —ISAIAH 61:1–3

1. Describe a fully formed worship ministry vision. Be specific in how the ministry is formed, how it expresses itself, and how the people relate to each other and the world.

_____

_____

_____

_____

_____

_____

_____

_____

_____

2. Pick a passage of Scripture where a prophet had vision for the future. Describe what the vision entailed.

_____

_____

_____

_____

3. What are two main themes of the Old Testament prophets' role as described in the metaphor section of this chapter?

_____

_____

_____

_____

WISDOM

1. What is a vision statement? Why is it helpful?

_____

_____

_____

_____

2. How do you think establishing a personal vision is helpful?

_____

_____

_____

_____

3. In Luke 4, Jesus presents his vision statement. What was his fivefold mission (see vv. 18–19)?

_____

_____

_____

_____

_____

4. After reading this week's chapter on "vision," list and explain below the six benefits of a worshiper practicing a life-based biblical vision.

_____

_____

_____

_____

_____

_____

5. How does a clear vision affect the worship leader's ministry, operationally? Why?

_____

_____

_____

_____

6. What does it mean to surrender your vision to God, and how does the Holy Spirit enable the worshiper to internalize this vision?

_____

_____

_____

_____

CHAPTER 26

COLLABORATION

No leader leads in a vacuum, there must be a
team that captures the leader's vision.

STORY

"Little John, come in. Little John, you there? Over. Little John, come in. You
at the put-in yet? Over."

The garbled transmission sounded from near John's feet in the raft just
as we left the shore and started our journey that morning.

John reached for his dry bag and pulled out a dingy yellow walkie-talkie.

"Already in. Going to be a fun run, Eighty-four. Over."

"Roger that. Early bird today. I like it. I'm thirty or so ahead and through
the boulder garden number one. Running high and smooth. I'll shout if there
are any surprises, but looking good so far. Over."

"Copy that. Catch ya soon, Eighty-four. Over and out."

John put the walkie-talkie back in his bag and pulled out a stick of
sunblock and started applying it to his nose.

"Eighty-four? Is that his name?" I asked.

"Nickname."

"Does he work for you guys?"

"No, he's a great friend and mentor-guide for another outfit. There are
several guiding companies in the area, but most of us that have been doing

it a while are part of a collective. We take turns scouting for each other. Lots
of incredible friendships have been formed in that group."

1. Think of a time when you needed guidance from a friend to learn something very
   important and significant.

   _____

   _____

   _____

   _____

   _____

   _____

2. Did you find that friend? If not, why not? And, what would you do to find such
   a friend? If you answered in the affirmative, would you say that your friend
   functioned more like a coach or mentor? Explain.

   _____

   _____

   _____

   _____

   _____

   _____

   _____

   _____

   _____

3. Are there special projects that you enjoy doing with at least one other person? If so,
   why do you think it is important to develop the team spirit? And, how do you and
   your friend(s) share in the assignments?

   _____

   _____

   _____

   _____

   _____

   _____

   _____

   _____

METAPHOR

Two people are better off than one, for they can help each other succeed. If one person falls, the other can reach out and help. But someone who falls alone is in real trouble. Likewise, two people lying close together can keep each other warm. But how can one be warm alone? A person standing alone can be attacked and defeated, but two can stand back-to-back and conquer. Three are even better, for a triple-braided cord is not easily broken.
—ECCLESIASTES 4:9–12 NLT

1. Why is collaboration foundational in the way of worship? Be specific—what does that look like for a group?

_____

_____

_____

_____

_____

_____

2. There is a tendency in life and leadership to ascend the mountain of life and work alone. Why do you think this approach to leadership could be very dangerous and be used as a tool of the evil one (Satan)?

_____

_____

_____

_____

_____

_____

John, our guide, found great joy in connecting with his fellow guides. They developed peer-to-peer, lifelong relationships. They lifted one another up and looked out for the safety and welfare of the other members. When John and Jimmy ("Eighty-four") exchanged messages over the walkie-talkie, it gave us all a window into the bigger picture. You could see the happiness on John's face to know that someone was out in front, scouting possible pitfalls and sharing the joys of the river.

3. The strength of working as a team is clearly beneficial to John, guide and hero of our story. List at least four reasons why this kind of team relationship could be beneficial to building a fully functional praise-and-worship team.

_____

_____

_____

_____

4. The demands of our schedules will drag us toward busyness and isolation. In what ways can the worship leader make it a priority to collaborate?

_____

_____

_____

_____

WISDOM

1. What is the difference between a partnership and collaboration?

_____

_____

_____

_____

2. How have you seen the "iron sharpens iron" principle at work in your life?

_____

_____

_____

_____

3. What are the five areas of collaboration discussed in this chapter?

    a. Collaboration with _____.

    b. Collaboration according to _____.

    c. Collaboration in _____.

    d. Collaboration in _____.

    e. Collaboration as a _____.

4. Why is unity important for collaboration?

_____

_____

_____

_____

5. Why is it important to seek out a collaborative team rather than going it alone?

_____

_____

_____

_____

6. What are the four critical parts of God's message in Acts 2:17? (Fill in the blanks.)

    a. God pours out his Spirit upon _____;

    b. The sons and daughters will _____;

    c. The young will have _____; and

    d. The old will dream _____.

7. Why is multigenerational worship important? What are the strengths and weaknesses in separating different generations for the purpose of practicing worship?

_____

_____

_____

_____

_____

CHAPTER 27

PERSEVERING

Stay the course. Finish well. Through the difficult
and tumultuous times, be faithful.

STORY

"The last big one of the day is just ahead, and it's a fun one!" John exclaimed.

"What's this one called, 'drown the fat guy' or 'city boy suckah'?" Neal said with a straight face.

It wasn't just what he said, it was how he said it that had us all in stitches. It was late afternoon, nearly dusk, and I found myself lamenting the idea of this trip ending. The beauty, the adventure, the new friends, the wildlife, the danger, the many facets of the river—it was unforgettable.

"That's hilarious, Neal! I may use one of those in the future. This one is actually called 'Chain-breaker Falls,'" John said.

"What's behind that name?" Leah asked.

"It's had that name long before we got here. My dad told me it's because, once you make it through, you realize there's nothing that can hold you back. You get a sense that you can accomplish anything. You're home free. Okay, lock in everyone, here we go! Forward hard!"

1. Are there areas in your life where you feel like you are not making forward progress? If yes, explain why. If no, explain how you are able to cope with the negative influences that would seek to distract you from success.

_____

_____

_____

_____

_____

_____

"I'm proud of you guys! What a great trip," John said as he pulled down the top of his wetsuit revealing his muscled torso in a tight tank top of sorts. An elaborate tattoo blanketed his right shoulder. It was a colorful intertwining of roses and thorns. At the top, the name 'Jenna Mae' in a cursive calligraphy font, and at the bottom, the words 'Forward Hard.'"

. . . "I actually have this tattoo for a couple of reasons. The first is to create something beautiful out of a nasty scar and the second is to remember Jenna Mae, my mom. She passed when I was twelve after a long fight with cancer."

None of us knew what to say.

"I lost my mom early too," Neal said.

"Can't get away from suffering, can you? She was an amazing lady. That was her phrase. Whenever things got difficult, she would say, 'Forward Hard.'" He looked down at the ink. "Suffering makes you real and makes you feel. Beauty is coming, but you've got to paddle through. Forward Hard."

2. What does it look like to implement the "forward hard" principle as a worshiper?

_____

_____

_____

_____

3. What three or four qualities should a worshiper have if they are going to exemplify a "forward hard" spirit?

_____

_____

_____

_____

4. List two or three areas in which you hope you can develop a "forward hard" spirit and attitude.

_____

_____

_____

_____

METAPHOR

Not only so, but we also glory in our sufferings, because we know that suffering produces perseverance; perseverance, character; and character, hope. And hope does not put us to shame, because God's love has been poured out into our hearts through the Holy Spirit, who has been given to us.
—ROMANS 5:3–5

1. What does it mean to you that Christ suffered on our behalf?

_____

_____

_____

_____

2. How have you seen suffering help you experience the power and presence of God?

_____

_____

_____

_____

3. What does Romans 5:3–5 teach the worshiper about God's grace and love?

_____

_____

_____

_____

4. In what ways does God's grace carry us through when it seems like things are just too hard?

_____

_____

_____

_____

_____

WISDOM

1. What four benefits are found in suffering for those who diligently seek to worship God?

_____

_____

_____

_____

2. How does God use suffering and brokenness to draw us to himself? Why is this important in building a relationship with God?

_____

_____

_____

_____

3. How do you think God uses the moments of suffering to reveal to us the most about himself?

_____

_____

_____

_____

4. Explain what this statement means: "Not one thing done for his glory is ever wasted."

_____

_____

_____

_____

5. How do you think suffering strengthens relationships?

_____

_____

_____

_____

6. If quitting is not an option for the worshiper, what assurance do we have that God will see us through the entire battle?

_____

_____

_____

_____

CHAPTER 28

PROCESS

Apprentice Guide, Master Guide, Mentor Guide.

STORY

"Okay everybody, we have reason to celebrate Anastasia today. She has successfully completed her journey as an apprentice and so shall be knighted a full-fledged guide this weekend!" John shouted.

Anastasia beamed as we clapped and cheered.

"Does this mean I don't have to take orders from you anymore?" she asked playfully.

"Nice try. I still sign your paycheck. Just because you're a guide doesn't mean you stop learning, young one."

We coasted gently down our last one hundred yards of river to enjoy. The sun descended behind the canyon walls and the air cooled. I drank it in as we crossed the calm waters to the take out. It was a day forever etched in my soul.

As we made our way across the gentle current, the gray-haired, bearded sage we met at the beginning of our trip was waiting with the van and trailer. He smiled and waved at us as we arrived.

"How'd we do, guys?" he asked in his low, raspy voice as he pulled our raft up onto the clay beach.

"Awesome!"

"Incredible!"

"A day I'll never forget!" We all responded in concert . . .

"Big John always tells us to keep the long view in mind. Each stage has its competencies and evaluations you have to pass. Once you're accepted into the program, you go from apprentice to guide, guide to master guide. From there, it's on to mentor guide. That means you are really multiplying yourself, training up other guides. Beyond that, I suppose it is just legendary status and you can't really measure that." Frankie glanced over to Big John as he worked. "The amazing thing is, the greatest legend of them all, the dude that has run more water and saved more lives than anyone, baked you cookies and is loading up your gear. Let that sink in! Being a legend isn't what you think."

1. What process do you think John is referring to as a river guide?

_____
_____
_____
_____
_____
_____
_____

2. What does "Big John" mean when he encourages everyone to "keep the long view in mind"? Why is this important individually and as a group?

_____
_____
_____
_____
_____
_____
_____

3. Who in your life are you seeking to "train up"?

_____
_____
_____
_____
_____
_____
_____

METAPHOR

Every time you cross my mind, I break out in exclamations of thanks to God. Each exclamation is a trigger to prayer. I find myself praying for you with a glad heart. I am so pleased that you have continued on in this with us, believing and proclaiming God's Message, from the day you heard it right up to the present. There has never been the slightest doubt in my mind that the God who started this great work in you would keep at it and bring it to a flourishing finish on the very day Christ Jesus appears.
—PHILIPPIANS 1:3–6 MSG

1. What process has God started and now must finish in your life?

_____
_____
_____
_____
_____
_____
_____

2. In what way are you growing in your faith, calling, and craft?

_____
_____
_____
_____
_____
_____
_____

3. What must you do to demonstrate your willingness to move by God's timetable and not your own?

_____
_____
_____
_____
_____
_____

WISDOM

1. How have you seen God shape and transform you for the way of worship?

_____
_____
_____
_____
_____

2. In your opinion, why does God want all hearts prepared and equipped for the task of living and leading worship?

_____
_____
_____
_____
_____
_____

3. Why is it important to remember that God is the one preparing each person for the task? And which task? Explain.

_____
_____
_____
_____
_____
_____

4. What do you think is the difference between "perfecting" and "establishing" us for service? In what ways is God perfecting and establishing you for service?

_____
_____
_____
_____

5. After carefully studying the chapter on "process," fill in the blank to list six ways God strengthens the worshiper:

I_____—giving insight, wisdom, articulation, courage, and words of encouragement.

P_____—making all of us stronger, providing endurance for the journey, and sustaining our health along the way.

E_____—bringing peace, rest, comfort, solitude, and affirmation during times of struggle.

M_____—granting abilities to comprehend, remember details, and recall concepts.

E_____—learning how to lead, learning how to follow, being equipped to stand and lead with confidence.

S_____—giving grace for success, faith to believe, and vision for tomorrow.

6. How are you allowing God to calm your spirit today?

_____

_____

_____

_____

EPILOGUE

Worship is the submission of all of our nature to God. It is the quickening of the conscience by his holiness; the nourishment of mind with his truth; the purifying of imagination by his beauty; the opening of the heart to his love; the surrender of will to his purpose—all this gathered up in adoration, the most selfless emotion of which our nature is capable.

—WILLIAM TEMPLE

1. How have you seen the power and presence of God guide you in your decisions?

_____

_____

_____

_____

2. What does it mean for you that leading worship is a lifelong journey?

_____

_____

_____

_____

3. What mountaintop or deep-valley experiences have helped you understand the importance of living your life with hope and gratitude?

_____

_____

_____

_____

4. In what ways has *The Way of Worship* enabled you to live a life full of adventure, exploration, discovery, peace, beauty, struggle, victory, or hope?

_____

_____

_____

_____

5. It is true that "we become like what or whom we worship." How are you seeking to be more like Christ?

_____

_____

_____

_____

6. As "worship guide," we are helping people experience who they were made for. How do you plan to help people experience Jesus in their life?

_____

_____

_____

_____

7. Summarize John 13:13–17 in your own words. Use the New International Version or the New King James Version of the Bible as a reference.

_____

_____

_____

_____

_____

WISDOM

1. What does it mean to you that worship is formational?

_____

_____

_____

_____

2. In what ways is worship transformational in your life?

_____

_____

_____

_____

3. In what ways do you demonstrate vertical and horizontal relationships?

_____

_____

_____

_____

4. Why do you think God calls worshipers to take worship of Jesus to the nations?

_____

_____

_____

_____

5. In what ways are you replicating what you've learned for other people?

_____

_____

_____

_____

NOTES

Introduction

1. "On that day the Lord made a covenant with Abram and said, "To your descendants I give this land, from the Wadi of Egypt to the great river, the Euphrates" (Genesis 15:18).
2. "But when she could hide him no longer, she got a papyrus basket for him and coated it with tar and pitch. Then she placed the child in it and put it among the reeds along the bank of the Nile" (Exodus 2:3).
3. "Behold, he drinketh up a river, and hasteth not: he trusteth that he can draw up Jordan into his mouth" (Job 40:23 KJV).
4. "He shall be like a tree planted by the rivers of water that bringeth forth his fruit in his season" (Psalm 1:3 KJV). "You feed them from the abundance of your own house, letting them drink from your river of delights" (Psalm 36:8 NLT). "There is a river, the streams whereof shall make glad the city of God, the holy place of the tabernacles of the most High" (Psalm 46:4 KJV).
5. "They will be like a tree planted by the water, that sends out its roots by the stream. It does not fear when heat comes; its leaves are always green. It has no worries in a year of drought and never fails to bear fruit" (Jeremiah 17:8). "And I saw in a vision; and it came to pass, when I saw, that I was at Shushan in the palace, which is in the province of Elam; and I saw in a vision, and I was by the river of Ulai" (Daniel 8:2 KJV) "Then I lifted up mine eyes, and saw, and, behold, there stood before the river a ram which had two horns: and the two horns were high; but one was higher than the other, and the higher came up last" (Daniel 8:3 KVJ).
6. "Then Jesus came from Galilee to the Jordan to be baptized by John" (Matthew 3:13).
7. "If anyone thirsts, let him come to Me and drink. He who believes in Me, as the Scripture has said, 'out of his heart will flow rivers of living water.' But this He spoke

concerning the Spirit, whom those believing in Him would receive" (John 7:37b–39 NKJV).

8. "And there went out unto him all the land of Judaea, and they of Jerusalem, and were all baptized of him in the river of Jordan, confessing their sins" (Mark 1:5 KJV).

9. "On the Sabbath we went outside the city gate to the river, where we expected to find a place of prayer. We sat down and began to speak to the women who had gathered there" (Acts 16:13).

10. "Then the angel showed me the river of the water of life, as clear as crystal, flowing from the throne of God and of the Lamb down the middle of the great street of the city" (Revelation 22:1–2).

Chapter 9: Character

1. Brett and Kate McKay, *A Man's Life, On Character, On Virtue*. June 25, 2013, updated November 27, 2018. https://www.artofmanliness.com/articles/what-is-character-its-3 -true-qualities-and-how-to-develop-it/ (accessed May 24, 2019).

2. Barrie Davenport, *Relationships*. https://liveboldandbloom.com/10/relationships/good -character-traits (accessed May 22, 2019).